Updated 2022

The Musical Aspects of the Ancient Egyptian Vocalic Language

Moustafa Gadalla

The Musical Aspects of
The Ancient Egyptian Vocalic Language
by Moustafa Gadalla

CONTENTS

1

ABOUT THE AUTHOR

Moustafa Gadalla is an Egyptian-American independent Egyptologist who was born in Cairo, Egypt in 1944. He holds a Bachelor of Science degree in civil engineering from Cairo University.

From his early childhood, Gadalla pursued his Ancient Egyptian roots with passion, through continuous study and research. Since 1990, he has dedicated and concentrated all his time to researching and writing.

Gadalla is the author of twenty-two published internationally acclaimed books about the various aspects of the Ancient Egyptian history and civilization and its influences worldwide. In addition he operates a multimedia resource center for accurate, educative studies of Ancient Egypt, presented in an engaging, practical, and interesting manner that appeals to the general public.

He was the Founder of Tehuti Research Foundation which was later incorporated into the multi-lingual Egyptian Wisdom Center (https://www.egyptianwisdomcenter.org) in more than ten languages. He is also the Founder and Head of the online Egyptian Mystical University (https://www.EgyptianMysticalUniversity.org). Another ongoing activity has been his creation and production of performing arts projects such as the Isis Rises Operetta (https://www.isisrisesoperetta.com); to be followed soon by Horus The Initiate Operetta; as well other productions.

2

PREFACE

This book will show the one-ness of the sound principles for both music and the Egyptian alphabetical vocalic language. It will show that the fundamentals, structure, formations, grammar, and syntax are exactly the same in music and in the Egyptian alphabetical vocalic language.

It is the aim of this book to provide such an exposition; one which, while based on sound scholarship, will present the issues in language comprehensible to non-specialist readers. Technical terms have been kept to a minimum. These are explained, as non-technically as possible, in the glossary.

This book is divided into 10 chapters.

Chapter 1: **Historical Deception of the (Ancient) Egyptian Linguistics** will clear the intended confusion to hide the alphabetical form of writing in Ancient Egypt as being the SOURCE of all languages throughout the world.

Chapter 2: **The Seamless Language and/of Music** covers

the unity of musical tones and Egyptian alphabet as well as the intimacy between language/speech/vocals and music in the Egyptian system.

Chapter 3: **The Human Vocal Instrument** covers the details of the human vocal generating system and its equivalence in musical instruments.

Chapter 4: **The Three Primary Tonal Sounds** covers the three primary rhythmic tones and their equivalence in the Egyptian three quantal vowels/sounds.

Chapter 5: **The Musical/Tonal/Tonic Alphabet** covers the letters of the Egyptian alphabet, being derived from the three primary tonal sounds/vowels, as well as the utilization of alphabet for musical instruments tonal notations.

Chapter 6: **Duality of Letters/Musical Tones** shows the dual nature of alphabetical letters and musical tones.

Chapter 7: **The "Atom" of Musical/Vocal Sounds** covers the fundamentals of generative phonology and the nature of the four sound variations of each letter and its exact equivalence in musical notes.

Chapter 8: **The Musical Rhythmic Sound Segmentation** covers the orderly sound segmentation in musical flow and its equivalence in syllables streams in all variations of length, duration, stress, junctures, boundaries, etc.

Chapter 9: **Harmonic/Rhythmic Word Formation/Morphology [Musical Triad]** covers the generative nature of both the musical triads and its equivalence in the Egyptian trilateral stem verbs.

Chapter 10: **Tonal/Musical Sentences & Their Types/ Various Forms [Themes and their variations]** covers the exact similarity between musical structural forms and sentence structures in grammar, syntax, semantics, functions and forms, etc.

Moustafa Gadalla

3

STANDARDS AND TERMINOLOGY

1. Throughout this book, octave ranges are named according to the following system:

c_3 c_2 c_1 c c^1 c^2 c^3

<— Lower Octaves –<—|—>– Higher Octaves—>

2. Capital letters (C, D, E, etc.) are reserved for general pitch names without regard to a specific octave range.

3. The Ancient Egyptian word, neter, and its feminine form netert, have been wrongly, and possibly intentionally, translated to 'god' and 'goddess' by almost all academics. Neteru (plural of neter/netert) are the divine principles and functions of the One Supreme God.

4. You may find variations in writing the same Ancient Egyptian term, such as Amen/Amon/Amun or Pir/Per. This is because the vowels you see in translated Egyptian texts are only approximations of sounds, which are used by Western Egyptologists to help them pronounce the Ancient Egyptian terms/words.

5. We will be using the most commonly recognized words for the English-speaking people that identify a neter/netert (god, goddess), a pharaoh, or a city; followed by other 'variations' of such a word/term.

It should be noted that the real names of the deities (gods, goddesses) were kept secret so as to guard the cosmic power of the deity. The Neteru were referred to by epithets that describe particular quality, attribute, and/or aspect(s) of their roles. Such applies to all common terms such as Isis, Osiris, Amun, Re, Horus, etc.

6. When using the Latin calendar, we will use the following terms:

> **BCE** – Before Common Era. Also noted in other references as BC.
> **CE** – Common Era. Also noted in other references as AD.

4

THE 28 ABGD LETTERS & PRONUNCIATIONS

– The actual Egyptian 28 ABGD letters are indicated in Capitals—non capitals letters are inserted to help English-speaking people pronounce the Egyptian words.

– When 2 letters are underlined together (in the "Roman" script), they represent one sound. For example: Th sounds like 'Th' in the English word 'Three'. Another example is Dh, which sounds like the Th' in the English word 'There'.

– An underlined letter followed by a dot indicates an Egyptian letter close to the English sound of such a letter.

– Three Egyptian letters [A, W & Y] are "weak consonants" – each can be pronounced as a consonant or a vowel sound, depending on the word and its context.

Letter Sound	Numerical Value	Letter sound in English words
1. **ALeF**	1	Adam (as a cons.), fat (as a vowel sound)
2. **BeYT**	2	Boy
3. **GyM**	3	Girl
4. **DaL**	4	Delta
5. **Heh**	5	He
6. **Waw**	6	We (as a cons. sound), FOOD (as a vowel sound)
7. **Zayn**	7	Zero
8. **H.et**	8	a strongly aspirant H made in the throat and is defined as a 'fricative faucal,' that is a strongly marked continuous guttural sound produced at the back of the palate. The sound does not exist in English, French, or Italian, but comes near to the ch in the German lachen, or the Scotch loch (Spanish x and j.)
9. **T.a**	9	emphatic T (close to the sound of double 't' at the end of the English word 'butt')
10. **Yad**	10	Yes (as a cons. sound), Feet (as a vowel sound), a semi-consonantal glide, like the y in "yellow"
11. **Kaf**	20	Milk
12. **Lam**	30	Lane
13. **Meem**	40	Milk
14. **Noon**	50	No
15. **Seen**	60	Safe

16. **A.yn**	70	does not occur in English, but represents a deeper guttural consonant, perhaps a voiced glottal stop
17. **F**	80	**F**ood
18. **S.ad**	90	emphatic S (close to the sound of letter 's' in the the English word 'sun' or in the name 'Sandra')
19. **Qaf**	100	It is defined as a 'hard. explosive ultra guttural,' and may be described as a guttural having an affinity with k, but formed further back, between the posterior soft portion of the palate and the back of the tongue. Sounds like a backward k; rather like q in queen
20. **R**	200	**R**ise
21. **Sheen**	300	**Sh**ow
22. **T**	400	**T**able
23. **Th**	500	**Th**ree
24. **Kh**	600	Gutteral Aspirate—like ch in Schotch loch—perhaps like ch in German ich
25. **Dhal**	700	O**Th**er
26. **D.ad**	800	emphatic D
27. **Z.**	900	emphatic Z
28. **Ghyn**	1000	A voiced velar fricative /ɣ/ or a voiced uvular fricative

5

MAP OF ANCIENT EGYPT

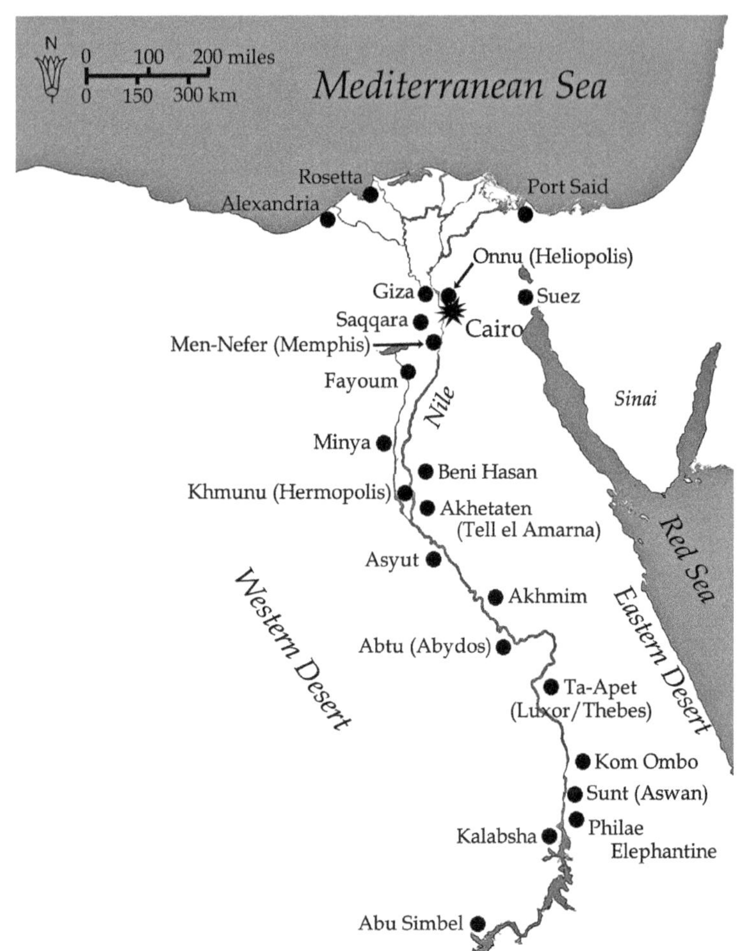
N
0 100 200 miles
0 150 300 km
Mediterranean Sea
Rosetta
Alexandria
Port Said
Onnu (Heliopolis)
Giza
Suez
Saqqara
Cairo
Men-Nefer (Memphis)
Fayoum
Nile
Sinai
Minya
Beni Hasan
Khmunu (Hermopolis)
Akhetaten
(Tell el Amarna)
Red Sea
Asyut
Western Desert
Akhmim
Eastern Desert
Abtu (Abydos)
Ta-Apet
(Luxor/Thebes)
Kom Ombo
Sunt (Aswan)
Philae
Elephantine
Kalabsha
Abu Simbel

Chapter 1 : Historical Deception of the (Ancient) Egyptian Linguistics

1.1 SMOKE SCREENING THOUSANDS OF EGYPTIAN ALPHABETICAL WRITINGS

The BIGGEST smoke screen in history is concealing the (Ancient) Egyptian alphabetical writing system. Scholars made everyone think of the Egyptian language as a collection of "primitive pictures" called hieroglyphics. They concealed the Egyptian alphabetical system as the MOTHER of ALL languages in the world.

Here is how Alan Gardiner, in his book *Egyptian Grammar,* tried to "rationalize" how they concealed the Egyptian alphabetical system:

> ***"Egyptologists have experienced the practical need of adopting some common standard to which different hieratic hands could be reduced, and instead of selecting one simple style of hieratic for the purpose, have preferred to transcribe all hieratic hands into hieroglyphic".***

Gardiner's "explanation/justification" for burying the Egyptian alphabetical [hieratic] writings assures that there were various forms of writings for various purposes. The very same Western academics NEVER used the same "lame excuse" with Greek, Roman, or any other language in the world. It is only the Egyptian alphabetical writing system that is concealed and replaced with arbitrary pictures, just because Ancient Egyptians—like everyone else—had different writing styles (?!).

This lame excuse was ONLY used in Egyptian writings to deceive others and conceal the Ancient Egyptian alphabetical writing language.

Furthermore, there is NOT A SINGLE reference prior to this 19th-20th century "Western Egyptologists' conspiracy that stated a relationship between hieroglyphics (pictorial signs) and hieratic/demotic (alphabetical letter-forms). On the contrary, EVERY Single reference stated EXPLICITLY how unrelated they are.

1.2 THE (ANCIENT) EGYPTIAN ALPHABETICAL FORM OF WRITING

The most eminent authority on languages, Isaac Taylor, in his book *History of the Alphabets* ,Volume 1, page 62, says:

> ***"The immensely early date at which symbols of an alphabetic nature are found on the Egyptian monuments is a fact of great interest and importance. It is of great interest, inasmuch as it constitutes the starting point in the history of the Alphabet, establishing the literal truth of the assertion that the letters of the***

> ***alphabet are older than the pyramids—older probably than any other existing monument of human civilization.***"

Isaac Taylor, in his book *History of the Alphabets,* Volume I, page 64, wrote about the Egyptian King Sent:

> ***"King Sent, in whose reign the alphabetic characters were already in use, may be taken to have lived between 4000 and 4700 BCE. Startling as the result of such calculations may appear, it must be affirmed to be probable that the beginnings of the graphic art in the valley of the Nile must be relegated to a date of seven or eight thousand years from the present time."***

It is very clear that the Ancient Egyptian alphabetical language was the FIRST in the world thousands of years prior the much-to-do-about nothing "Sinai scripts."

The more one studies the various languages (and dialects) in the world, the more it becomes clearer and clearer that there was originally one language that split into various tongues. The Bible and ancient writers affirm such an original language. Because of false pride and the prejudices of Western academia and religious (Judaism, Christianity, and Islam) zealots, the origin of this universal mother language has been ignored.

Evidence confirms that Ancient Egypt is the single source of the universal language. On this subject matter, Plato admits the role of Egypt in his Collected Dialogues [*Philebus* 18-b, c, d]. For now, we shall only refer to the recognition of the Egyptian alphabetical letters as indicative of the unity of speech and script. In *Philebus* [18-d]:

> ***"...he [the Ancient Egyptian Theuth (Thoth)] conceived of 'letter' as a kind of bond of unity, uniting as it were all these sounds into one, and so he gave utterance to the expression 'art of letters,' implying that there was one art that dealt with the sounds."***

The reference to Theuth above is the same Theuth mentioned in the Phaedrus, where we are explicitly told that he was an Ancient Egyptian neter (god), ***'the one whose sacred bird is called the Ibis'*** so as to exclude all doubt about his identity. It is obvious that his account is based on a genuine Egyptian tradition, because the ibis-headed Theuth (Thoth) is an Egyptian neter (god).

It is very clear that Plato (in *Philebus* [18-b, c, d]) did not refer to pictorial forms of expression (hieroglyphs), but rather to expression by individual and diverse letters, each with its particular sound value. Other classical writers also stated that Egypt was the original source of alphabets. Contrary to facts, the Phoenicians were given the credit of inventing alphabets!

Most modern Western scholars affirm, both explicitly and implicitly, that the Ancient Egyptian alphabet (and language) is the oldest source in the world. In his book

The Literature of the Ancient Egyptians [page xxxiv-v], the German Egyptologist Adolf Erman admits:

> ***"The Egyptians alone were destined to adopt a remarkable method, following which they attained to the highest form of writing, the alphabet. . ."***

The British Egyptologist W.M. Flinders Petrie, in his book *The Formation of the Alphabets* [page 3], concluded:

> ***"From the beginning of the prehistoric ages, a cursive system consisting of linear signs, full of variety and distinction was certainly used in Egypt."***

Petrie has collected and tabulated alphabetical letter-forms from very different ages. The earliest belong to the early prehistoric age of Egypt, probably before 7000 BCE, and extends to the Greek and Roman Eras. Petrie also compiled (from several independent sources) similar-looking alphabetical letter-forms from 25 locations in Asia Minor, Greece, Italy, Spain, and other locations throughout Europe. All are dated centuries after the Ancient Egyptian alphabetical letter-forms.

Petrie's tabulation of these alphabetical letter-forms shows that:

1. All alphabetical letter-forms were present in Ancient Egypt since early pre-dynastic eras over 7,000 years ago, prior to anyplace else in the world.

2. All the Egyptian alphabetical-letter forms are clearly distinguishable in the oldest recovered, so-called Egyptian "hieratic writing" more than 5,000 years ago.

3. The same exact Ancient Egyptian letter-forms were later adopted and spread by other people throughout the world.

The Ancient Egyptian texts reflect the high culture of the Egyptian language and people. The German Egyptologist Adolf Erman, in his book *The Literature of the Ancient Egyptians* [page xxiv], wrote:

> ***"As far back as we can trace it, the Egyptian language displays signs of being carefully fostered. It is rich in metaphors and figures of speech, a "cultured language", which "composes and thinks" for the person who writes."***

The British Egyptologist Alan Gardiner, in his book *Egyptian Grammar* [page 4], wrote:

> ***"No less salient a characteristic of the language is its concision; the phrases and sentences are brief and to the point. Involved constructions and lengthy periods are rare, though such are found in some legal documents. The vocabulary was very rich. The clarity of Egyptian is much aided by a strict word-order…"***

> ***"For pithiness of proverbs, oracles and sentences, no language can parallel with it.***

> ***In axioms, maxims and aphorisms, it is excellent above all other languages.***

> ***For definitions, divisions and distinctions, no language is so apt."***

1.3 EGYPTIAN IS DEAD—LONG LIVE "ARABIC"

After concealing the (Ancient) Egyptian alphabetical writing system that makes everyone think of the Egyptian language as a collection of "primitive pictures" called 'hieroglyphics', the second blow was declaring that the Ancient Egyptian language is DEAD, and was replaced—out of thin air—by the "Arabic" language!

To say that Egyptians "speak Arabic" is totally false and illogical. It is the other way around—the "Arabs" have long ago "adopted" and continue to speak EGYPTIAN.

The British Egyptologist Alan Gardiner, in his book *Egyptian Grammar*, page 3, writes:

> ***"The entire vocalic system of Old Egyptian may indeed be proved to have reached a stage resembling that of Hebrew or modern Arabic"***

Egyptian is the mother of all Semitic languages, as proven and concluded by ALL academicians.

More details and information are given in *The Ancient Egyptian Universal Writing Modes* by Moustafa Gadalla.

Chapter 2 : The Seamless Language and/of Music

2.1 LANGUAGE AND/OF MUSIC

Rational meanings or values are naturally inherent in the spoken letters of the alphabet and their corresponding sounds, irrespective of usage, by reason of the structure of the instrument of speech, in the same way as musical values are inherent in the notes of a piano.

A typical letter-sound, valued rationally and not subjectively, is a natural sign, via the physical audition and the sound-waves, of the corresponding letter-production by the speech-instrument; and therefore has a similar character.

The structure of speech is comparable to the structure of a piano as the inherent means of producing different musical values as sound. Not letters, but letter sounds, were therefore 'natural signs', by this account.

The Egyptians perceived language and music as being two sides of the same coin. Both poetry and singing followed similar rules for musical composition. Poetry is written not only with a rhyme scheme, but also with a recurring pattern of accented and unaccented syllables. Each syllable alternates between accented and unaccented, making a double/quadruple meter and several other varieties. Patterns of set rhythms or lengths of phrases of Ancient Egyptian poems, praises, hymns, and songs of all kinds, which are known to have been chanted or performed with some musical accompaniment, were rhythmic, with uniform meters and a structured rhyme.

2.2 THE EGYPTIAN TONAL WRITING SYSTEM

The Egyptian language has had a natural, organized, comprehensive, and coherent system for representing all the qualities of its tonal aspects which are implemented in speech, poetry, singing, and musical performances.

The written forms were/are composed of two primary elements:

1. Letter-forms as symbols and sounds.

2. Associated with the Ancient Egyptian alphabetical letters proper are a number of complimentary symbols which serve to modulate or regulate part or the whole of their sound-value. Similarly bilateral and similarly trilateral syllables are almost always accompanied by such signs. Such signs used in this way are called 'phonetic complements'. As noted by all Egyptologists, the ***"complete absence of phonetic complements is uncommon."***

   Not only do these phonetic notations have tonal function, but just as important, they have syntactical function. In the Egyptian language, syntactical and tonal functions are ONE AND THE SAME.

The phonetic notations/signs serve three functions:

1. Syntax—to provide information on the syntactical structure of the text. They divide verses into smaller units of meaning, a function which also gives them a limited (but sometimes important) role as a source for exegesis. This function is accomplished through the use of various conjunctive signs (which indicate that words should be connected in a single phrase) and especially in a hierarchy of dividing signs of various strengths, which divide each verse into smaller phrases.

The function of the disjunctive notations/signs may be roughly compared to modern punctuation signs such as periods, commas, semicolons, etc.

2. Phonetics—to indicate the specific syllable where the stress (accent) falls in the pronunciation of a word.

3. Music—as the phonetic notations/signs have musical value, reading the text with them becomes a musical chant where the music itself serves as a tool to emphasize the proper accentuation and syntax (as mentioned previously).

These phonetic markings are generally smaller-size letters. The addition of a line, dot, or hooked curve modified the basic term with respect to gender, number, person, tense, voice, or other grammatical categories, depending on where it was placed (above, below, left or right and so forth).

Notations (phonetic and tonic markings) reveal the musicality/melodic of texts.

The practice of indicating the pronunciation by writing furigana alongside the characters depends on the purpose of writing, the level of expected pronunciation accuracy, and who will be the expected reader. For example: you will not find it in newspapers, but you *will* find the supplementary phonetic symbols being used, to varying degrees, in some books; epecially in religious texts and texts where musicality is essential, such as chanting.

Notation in Egypt was employed as far back as the 28th century BCE.

François Joseph Fétis, an accomplished musicologist, discovered the roots of the Greeks' notation symbols to be the demotic form of the Ancient Egyptian writing. F.J. Fétis states, in his *Biographie Universelle des Musiciens et Bibliographie Générale de la Musique* [Bruxelles, 1837, tome I, p. lxxi.]:

> ***"I have not the least doubt, that this musical notation [used in ecclesiastical music by the modern Greeks] belonged to ancient Egypt. I have in support of my opinion the resemblance borne by the signs in this notation, erroneously attributed to St. John of Damascus, to those of the demotic, or popular characters of the ancient Egyptians. . ."***

M. Fétis continued by pointing out the resemblance between numerous symbols employed by the Greeks to determine the duration of notes, and certain characters of the Egyptian demotic symbols, in a lengthy and detailed analysis [read more of the portion of the English translation of M. Fétis's text in Carl Engel's book, *The Music of the Most Ancient Nations*, pages 271-2]. M. Fétis did not hesitate to conclude:

> ***"After this detailed analysis of the system of notation employed in the music of the Greek Church, and after comparing its signs with those of the demotic character in use among the Egyptians, can we for a moment doubt that the invention of this notation is to be ascribed to that ancient people [the Egyptians], and not to St. John of Damascus. . ."***

M. Fétis's detailed analysis and conclusion proves, beyond the shadow of any doubt, that the Greeks borrowed the musical notation of the Egyptian demotic symbols.

2.3 SIGNIFICANCE OF MUSICALITY IN ANCIENT EGYPT

Words and language are pervaded by an essential music through the letters and their relations, underlying the highly variable emotional or aesthetic values of tone, pitch, and stress introduced by the voice and the manner of articulation. Furthermore, the typical letter-frequencies and resultant audible vibrations in the instrument of hearing carry the rational values equivalent to the natural letter meanings so that the essential music must have a direct correspondence to the essential poetry which results from these meanings.

Emphasis on the written text is predominant in Egypt, but they also engage the acoustic dimension of language in ways that bring it into alliance with recitation techniques and sonorous iconography.

Given the importance of chants, spells, and a person's name in Ancient Egypt, it is clear that the sound of the words must have had a functional connection with their meanings. For them, speaking was a process of generating sonar fields, establishing an immediate vibratory identity with the essential principle that underlies any object or form. Chanting in prescribed rhythm(s) was important during temple rituals, medical procedures, and the administration of medicine, as well as for the deceased's funerary rites.

To the mutual assimilations of vocal and instrumental melodies of speech and of music, we could easily add the case of common cantillation in the liturgy of Egypt, where the transition from speaking to singing and back to language is so continuous that a definite line of demarcation cannot be drawn. The Egyptians have, in their speech enunciation, a distinct trend towards musical intonation.

Next, we begin with Sound Producers…

Chapter 3 : The Human Vocal Instrument

3.1 VOCAL MUSIC THEMES

As shown earlier, the Egyptians perceived language and music as being two sides of the same coin. Each letter has its own musical form, with its own particular energy. Words and phrases must be composed in the same manner as musical compositions by the careful threading of selected notes/ letters.

Patterns of set rhythms or lengths of phrases of Ancient Egyptian poems, praises, hymns, and songs of all kinds, which are known to have been chanted or performed with some musical accompaniment, were rhythmic, with uniform meters and a structured rhyme.

Ancient Egyptian texts show that Egyptians spoke and sang in musical patterns on all occasions and for all purposes, from the most sacred to the most mundane. Present-day Egyptians are like their ancestors—they love to sing about anything and everything. There is nothing that is too insignificant or too large to sing a song to (or about).

The treasure of songs included simple workers' calls or extended songs performed in all types of occupations, such as by farmers, fishermen, and artisans. All various occasions had their appropriate songs, such as lamentations and songs to the deceased; hymns, litanies, and entertainment songs of philosophical content; love songs; festive songs during the Nile floods; the Egyptian New Year celebration; sung and recited prayers or spells in honor of the neteru (gods, goddesses); songs to welcome the morning sun, etc. Each type of song had/has its appropriate mode/melody to suit the occasion, either of rejoicing and festivity, solemnity, or lamentation.

In general, there are eight types of graduated vocal music, from the pure non-musical word (plain talking) to the pure music which Egyptians (Ancient and Sufi) master. The shades graduated from monotone poetry, recitative, and chant, to ultimately pure musical vocalization, with no literary context.

3.2 GENERATING VOCAL SOUNDS

The physiological-anatomical components of the speech mechanism are the vocal tract components and the multichannel auditory monitoring system (ears).

The most basic of all musical instruments is the human voice. The human voice was/is the instrument par excellence of the priest and the enchanter in Ancient Egypt. The typical gesture of the Egyptian singer has always been, since ancient times, to put one or both his hands to his ear(s), to control/regulate the pitch of his singing. This gesture serves to fortify the sound, because the singer may hear his voice louder, stronger, and even slightly changed.

The Egyptian (Ancient and present-day Sufi) singer was/is well-trained to generate the widest compass, variation, and articulation of sounds by utilizing the four agents that cooperate in producing the needed tones, with particular sections of pitch, loudness, and timbre. They are:

1. Wind Supply. This is accomplished by the proper breathing techniques. The breathing cycle, in-out-rest and tension-relaxation-balance, are all critical to the success of the music. Breathing lies at the root of rhythm and phrasing. Breath is the basis of speech, and therefore its control is essential to good speech.

2. Tone Producer. The vocal cords are the actual tone producer. They are a pair of muscles in the larynx that set up the primary vibration. The vibration is started by an air stream sent against them from the lungs.

3. Amplifiers. The bones and cavities throughout the head and the upper part of the body participate in resonating the sound to provide amplification.

Accordingly, one speaks of a head tone and a chest tone. Head resonance favors the high overtones. Chest resonance favors the lower overtones. The correct ratio of these two main resonators, to each other, accounts for a clear, bright, and free tone. Both adjust to each other all the time, and function simultaneously.

4. Articulators. Articulation of the sound is accomplished by the activity of the mouth and all its components. The articulators are the vocal tract structures involved in the movements used to produce speech sounds. By definition, the word "articulate" implies movement.

3.3 HUMAN-LIKE MUSICAL INSTRUMENTS

There are two spices of human voice—intervallic and continuous.

It is agreed by all sides that the construction of the organs of speech so far resemble a reed organ-pipe; that sound is generated by a vibratory apparatus in the larynx, answering to the reed, by which the pitch or number of vibrations in a given time is determined; and that this sound is afterwards modified and altered in its quality by the cavities of the mouth and nose, which answer to the pipe that organ builders attach to the reed for a similar purpose.

Such instruments are classified according to the means of producing the vibration. The most usual means of exciting the vibrations of a column of air in a pipe is by blowing into, or rather, over it; either at its open end or at an orifice made for the purpose at the side, or by introducing a small current of air into it through an aperture of a peculiar construction called a reed. This is provided with a "tongue," or flexible elastic plate, which nearly stops the aperture, and which is alternately forced away by the current of air and returns by its elasticity. Thus, it produces a continual and regularly periodic series of interruptions to the uniformity of the stream and, of course, a sound in the pipe corresponding to their frequency – except, however, that the reed must be so constructed as to be capable of vibrating in unison, or nearly so, with at least one of the modes of vibration of the column of air in the pipe. Otherwise, the sound of the reed only will be heard, the resonance of the pipe will not be called into play, and the pipe will not speak (or will speak, but only feebly and imperfectly, and will yield a false tone).

The Egyptians have long been using musical instruments that can follow the same spices of voice—intervallic and continuous. Most significant among them are:

- Single Reed Pipe (Clarinet)
- Double Pipe—including bagpipe and Organ

Single Reed Pipe (Clarinet)

Egyptian pipes of all kinds were/are made from reed plants, which are abundant near Egyptian irrigation canals.

The Egyptian single reed pipe (clarinet) contains a reed near the mouth that vibrates when one blows directly into the hole, through the pipe. The breath is directed through a wooden or ivory beak onto a sharp "lip" cut in the pipe itself.

The Egyptian single reed pipe is of equal antiquity as the nay (flute). It was a straight tube, without any increase at the mouthpiece. The reed pipes differ from the nay in construction, such as length, number of holes, etc.

Several Egyptian single reed pipes are found in museums throughout the world.

Pipes had/have equidistant finger holes. In order to produce a musical scale, the performer must control the size of the hole, the breath, the fingering, or by other special playing techniques.

Double Pipes

Numerous Ancient Egyptian reed pipes and double pipes were recovered from tombs and are now scattered in museums all over the world. The double pipes in Ancient Egypt had different kinds. Some had only one mouth hole, and others two, but were placed so near together as to enable the performer to blow upon both pipes at the same time. The mouthpiece of a pipe consists of a thin tube, closed at the upper end. A tongue is cut into the tube, and vibrates in the player's mouth.

The pipes are either of equal length, or one is shorter than the other. They are blown simultaneously and played in unison. Sometimes one pipe has finger holes while the other does not. Sometimes one pipe served as a drone accompaniment, and its holes were stopped with wax. The Egyptians occasionally inserted little pegs or tubes into some of the finger holes to regulate the order of intervals or the mode in which they intended to perform.

As the placement of the finger holes (and hence the tones) do not completely correspond to one another, there are certain lingering effects, as well as sharper and more penetrating tones, than is the case with ordinary instruments. This drone playing is confirmed from three facts: the peculiar arrangement of the players' fingers in Egyptian art works; the present practice in Egypt; and the excavation of a pipe with all except one finger hole stopped with wax.

Pipes with many finger holes were used for the playing of melodies, while others were used for the production of an accompanying tone similar to the drone of the bagpipe. As such, the double pipe allows different playing types:

1. alternate playing
2. octave playing
3. a melody with a "pedal" either below or above
4. "Duet playing", the simultaneous performance of two melodies whether rhythmically distinct or allied.

For more detailed and fully illustrated information about the different types of double pipes of Ancient (and present-day) Egypt, read *The Enduring Ancient Egyptian Musical System* by Moustafa Gadalla.

Chapter 4 : The Three Primary Tonal Sounds

4.1 THE THREE PRIMARY RHYTHMIC TONES

Everything in the universe, large or small, has its own rhythm. Rhythm means flow: a movement that surges and recedes in intensity; and water is the best physical representation of flow.

In their typical story form fashion, the Ancient Egyptians described the major aspects of music, its laws, cosmic connections, etc., as it relates to the seasonal changes of the Nile River and not climatic changes.

In his *Book I* [Section 16-1], Diodorus of Sicily states:

> ***"It was by Thoth [Tehuti], according to ancient Egyptians. . . [who] was the first to observe the orderly arrangement of the stars and the harmony of the musical sounds and their nature.***
>
> ***He also made a lyre that has three tones, a high, a low, and a medium; to correspond to the three seasons of the Egyptian year."***

Lyre means the musical system and the instrument on which to study the system.

4.2 THE THREE QUANTAL VOWELS/SOUNDS

For the three water-related tones—high, low and medium— the Ancient Egyptian vocalic language has had three equivalent primary vowels:

- High, being the letter/vowel A—as in mad
- Low, being the letter/vowel Y /I—as in me
- Medium, being the letter/vowel W/O/U—as in moo

These three sounds, considered in relation to the human organs of speech, correspond respectively to the greatest diminution of the aperture of the throat by means of the tongue to nearly the greatest diminution of the external orifice of the mouth by means of the lips, and to nearly the greatest opening of the mouth and throat.

These three primary quantal vowels are unique in several ways:

1. First, they are present (or were historically) in the sound patterns of the vast majority of human languages.

2. Second, these vowels represent extreme positions of the tongue, with tight constrictions in each of three widely separate regions of the vocal tract: palatal, velar, and pharyngeal.

3. Third, apes, most fossil hominids, and newborn infants cannot make these three "extreme" vowels because they do not have a two-tube resonating system. In itself that might not be extraordinary; but [Y/I, A, W/O/U/] are special or quantal in nature. They

can be produced only if the vocal tract is tightly constricted in such a way as to form two tubes.

> – For [Y/I], the oral cavity is tightly constricted and the pharyngeal cavity is expanded.
> – For [A], the opposite holds: The oral cavity is fully expanded and the pharyngeal tube is tightly constricted.
> – For [W/O/U], the oral cavity is slightly more expanded than the pharyngeal cavity, with a tight constriction between the two tubes.

For all three vowels, there are sharp changes in vocal tract size near the midpoint of the vocal tract. It is this midpoint discontinuity in the two-tube vocal tract of humans that permits quantal vowel sounds to be produced.

Any speaker can be relatively imprecise in positioning the tongue and jaw for these three vowels. That is, sloppy articulation still produces reasonably good acoustic approximations of these three vowels.

Quantal vowel sounds are satisfactory for communication in many ways.

1. First, they are acoustically powerful and can carry hundreds of yards in the open air.

2. Second, since only a quasi-human vocal tract can produce them, hearing them would indicate a human signal, rather than that of prey or predator.

3. Third, rapid, efficient speech production involves the swift articulation of streams of syllables. Since each syllable generally contains a vocalic (vowel-like)

> nucleus, they could serve as the basis for an efficient, syllable-based speech production code.

It is from these three Ancient Egyptian-identified primary/basic sounds/pitches/tones that ALL sounds are created, as will be shown next.

Chapter 5 : The Musical/ Tonal/Tonic Alphabets

5.1 LETTERS—DERIVATIVES OF THE 3 QUANTAL VOWELS

As indicated earlier, the primary/quantal (or so-called "simple") vowels are identified, by Egyptologists, as being used by Ancient Egyptians thousands of years before the "Phoenicians" (as: A, Y & W).

These three letters indicate the central and two extreme positions of the action of parts of the mouth upon the voice. But between these extreme positions lie an infinite number of others, and the subtlety of our organs is such that we are able to glide, by almost imperceptible degrees, from one position to another, and each position will, of course, correspond to a different modification of the voice.

The stoppage of the finger along a musical string is equivalent to consonants that can be produced vocally. In other words, the vowels are the primary sounds and "consonants" are merely from stopping of the flow of the vowel sound at a certain way, in our human vocal system.

5.2 THE 25 ARTICULATED ALPHABETICAL/ MUSICAL LETTERS

Richard A. Firmage, in his book *The Alphabet ABECEDARIUM: Some Notes on Letters,* page 288, states:

> ***"The theoretical ideal goal of an alphabet is to reproduce every shade of sound with the greatest possible exactitude."***

Speech is a succession of sound, each one being an individual unit. Each sound is due to one impulse given to the air by the vocal organs, and the first and most obvious way of representing these sounds would be to have a separate character for each separate sound – that is, a sign that should direct anyone who sees it that he is to give the air a similar impulse. The number of these characters would be immense, and some means would have to be devised for reducing it. Such modern scientific logical thinking exactly followed the Ancient Egyptian system, as admitted and explained in Plato's *Collected Dialogues* in *Philebus* [18-b, c, d]:

> ***"SOCRATES: The unlimited variety of sound was once discerned by some god, or perhaps some godlike man; you know the story that there was some such person in Egypt called Theuth.***
>
> ***He it was who originally discerned the existence, in that unlimited variety, of:***
>
> ***-the vowels—not 'vowel' in the singular but 'vowels' in the plural—and then of***
>
> ***-other things which, though they could not be called***

articulate sounds, yet were noises of a kind. There were a number of them too, not just one, and

-as a third class he discriminated what we now call the mutes.

Having done that, he divided up the noiseless ones or mutes until he got each one by itself, and did the same thing with the vowels and the intermediate sounds; in the end he found a number of the things, and affixed to the whole collection, as to each single member of it, the name 'letter.'

It was because he realized that none of us could ever get to know one of the collection all by itself, in isolation from all the rest, that he conceived of 'letter' as a kind of bond of unity, uniting as it were all these sounds into one, and so he gave utterance to the expression 'art of letters,' implying that there was one art that dealt with the sounds."

The reference to Theuth above is the same Theuth mentioned in Phaedrus, where we are explicitly told that he was an Ancient Egyptian neter (god); ***"the one whose sacred bird is called the Ibis"***, so as to exclude all doubt about his identity. It is obvious that his account is based on a genuine Egyptian tradition, because the ibis-headed Thoth (Tehuti) is an Egyptian neter (god).

Plato, in *Philebus* [18-b, c, d], tells us (in his obscure way) that:

1. The Egyptian Theuth (Thoth/Tehuti) was the first to observe the infinity of sound.

2. Theuth (Thoth/Tehuti) divided up the infinity of sound into three distinct categories: regular vibrations (pitch), random vibrations (noise), and the absence of sound (muting).

Mutation is the separation/differentiation in time and space between the different tones. Without proper mutations, we have chaos. The proper separation of sounds enables us to distinguish and recognize each sound and how the consecutive sounds relate to each other. In other words, mutation identifies the distance/time between two sounds: the interval.

Mutations also set the different rhythmic patterns—the different tempos.

3. Theuth (Thoth/Tehuti) set the principle of the written language—letters—as graphic representations (images/pictures) of spoken/sound vibrations.

Thoth represents the Divine Messenger who articulates and writes the spoken/written language, knowledge, etc.

Thoth is portrayed as an ibis-headed figure, writing on a tablet.

Several of Thoth (Tehuti)'s attributes were confirmed by Diodorus of Sicily:

> ***"It was by Thoth (Tehuti), according to Ancient Egyptians, that the common language of mankind was first further articulated, and that many objects which were still nameless received an appellation, that the alphabet were defined, and that ordinances regarding the honors and offerings due to the neteru (gods) were duly***

> ***established; he was the first also to observe the orderly arrangement of the stars and the harmony of the musical sounds and their nature.*** " *Book I*, Section 16-1

The Ancient Egyptians called their language Medu Neter, meaning 'words of neter (god)'. The Egyptian term is indicative of the unity of speech and script; i.e. sound and form.

Plato's *Collected Dialogues* affirms the Ancient Egyptians' intent of their language, in Philebus [18-d]:

> ***"...he [the Ancient Egyptian Theuth[Thoth] conceived of 'letter' as a kind of bond of unity, uniting as it were all these sounds into one, and so he gave utterance to the expression 'art of letters,' implying that there was one art that dealt with the sounds."***

The Ancient Egyptian alphabet consists of 28 letters: 25 articulated letters in addition to the three primary/quantal vowels. Plutarch told us of such in *Moralia Vol. V*, [56 A]:

> ***"Five makes a square of itself, as many as the letters of the Egyptian alphabet."***

The three primary/quantary vowels A, Y, and W were not counted in the number of the 25 consonants/letters because they were/are not produced by human articulating organs. Such practice was universal at that time. Moreover, it continues to be endorsed by modern-day linguists.

5.3 ALPHABETICAL LETTERS AS WRITTEN MUSICAL NOTES

In general, notations for musical instruments were indicated as 1) a companion to the singing syllables as well as alternating with vocals, or 2) music without singing.

1) Accompaniment to Vocals

In order to minimize confusion between the text syllables and accompanying music, musical notations are shown as alphabetical letter-forms in various positions—mutilated, barred, lengthened, doubled, etc.

The second and fifth degrees/notes of the scale, B and H (E), were given 2 symbols each. All other notes of the diatonic scale had three symbols – or rather, one letter written in 3 positions: erect, prone and reversed.

Erect signs designated the diatonic naturals (corresponding to our white keys), and both the flattened and reversed signs meant sharps, representing smaller intervals such as 1/4,1/3,3/8 tones (enharmonic notes).

Barred musical symbols operate in conjunction with text syllables. Certain notes sometimes appear with a bar above them or through them (¥), signifying a portion of a natural note. The barred symbols appear above short syllables in several places, as well as above the second element of the divided long vowel. The bar means that the same note is sung, but in a different way; or with some difference in musical accompaniment.

2) Music Alone

Individual notes were indicated by alphabetical letter-forms. Each degree of the scale was represented by a letter of the alphabet, used purely for musical instruments.

Letters were used to signify the seven natural tones of the diatonic scale, and each of the seven original notes of the scale was followed by two supplementary notes for smaller intervals, such as 1/4,1/3, and 3/8 tones—enharmonic notes.

Chapter 6 : Duality of Letters/Musical Tones

6.1 DUALITY OF LETTERS—VOICED AND UNVOICED

Phonetic analysis implicitly recognizes a number of phonetic features that distinguish broad classes of elements. For example, consonants fall into two major classes: those that are voiced, and those that are voiceless. This in turn implies a binary distinctive feature. Many phonological distinctions are naturally binary, in the sense that some physiological gesture is either present in or absent from any given phonological element.

On a practical level, lip readers learn to realize that consonants are distinguished into pairs, having the same formation on the lips; but one is vocal and the other is not. For example, 'd' and 't', and 'z' and 's' look the same when spoken and present difficulties to the lip reader, but the difference can usually be read by the context.

Such phenomena are found clearly in the 28 letters of the Egyptian language. It must be noted that Egyptians are the only people in the "Arabic" speaking countries who can distinctively pronounce all 28 sounds—because it is their language, after all.

In the Egyptian Sufi traditions, the 28 ABGD letters are also divided into twin-letter classes of "bright" and "dark".

6.2 DUALITY OF MUSICAL TONES—AUTHENTIC & PLAGAL

The very same binary distinction in the 28 Egyptian alphabetical letters are also found in harmonic musical sounds.

It is recognized that each natural musical tone has a mirror image (complementary opposite) tone at a specific and 'consistent ratio'. By a shift of this specific ratio in the internal structure of any musical scale, it will produce its "*Siamese twin*" scale. The 2-octave scale is a twin scale: one is based on a sequence of natural tones and the other is based on the sequence of their opposite notes. In Western terms, the twin scales are called "plagal" and "authentic"!!

But what is this 'consistent musical ratio'? It is the Egyptian musical unit known as the 'comma', and has the value of 22.6415 cents. (A cent is a standard unit for measuring musical intervals. An octave is equal to 1,200 cents.) More about measuring units in music and speech is in the next chapter.

Chapter 7 : The "Atom" of Musical/Vocal Sounds

7.1 THE MUSICAL MEASURING UNIT—NATURAL PROGRESSION

We have just highlighted the phenomena of the twin octave with their mirror image twin-tones. We have also indicated that the difference in vibrations between a note and its complementary opposite is always 22.6415 cents—known as the Egyptian musical comma. This particular number is the natural result of both the theory and practice of playing musical instruments, as we will see next.

First we begin the theory by examining the sequence of the 'cycle of fifths.'

All musical scales are generated through the (geometric) progression of the Fifth.

The seven tones of the diatonic scale (Do, Re, Mi, Fa, Sol, La, Si) are the result of three progressions of Fifths. To simplify matters, we will illustrate the three progressions of the Fifth on the keyboard, as follows:

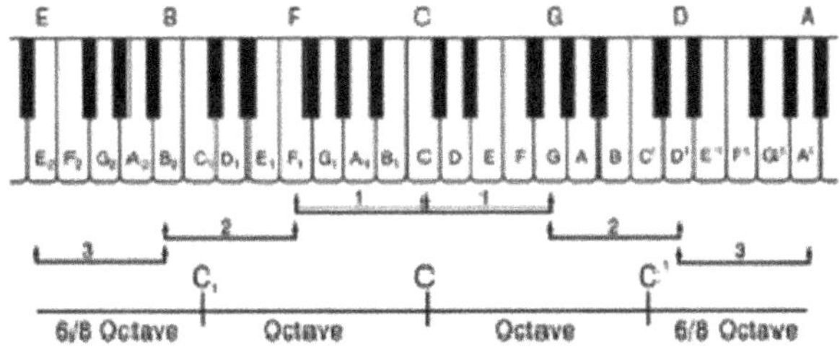

1. If we begin at any musical note (say, the middle C (Do), as a generator), we then find its two reciprocal Fifths, as shown above (F and G).

2. The second progression (from F and G) generates two more reciprocal Fifths (B and D), from the above two Fifths. This results in the pentatonic scale.

3. The third progression (from B and D) comes from adding two more reciprocal Fifths (E and A),and the heptatonic scale is obtained.

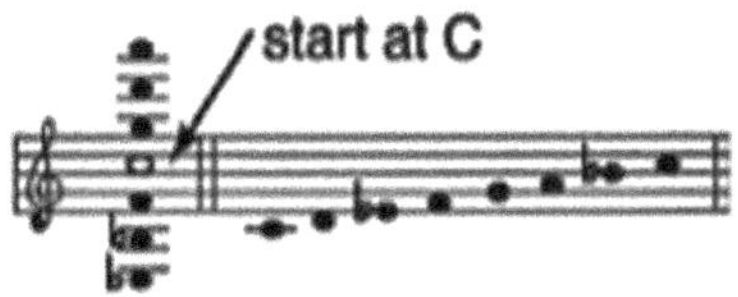

The diatonic scale is thus formed from any seven adjacent terms of a geometric series, ruled by the constant $^3/_2$ or $^2/_3$—the proportion of the Perfect Fifth. The seven natural musical tones are therefore obtained from the generative operation that extend three times, but no more.

To illustrate the cycle of consecutive Fifths, which produce the diatonic scale on the keyboard, we imagine that the tones along the top line (E B F C G D A) are made into a circle with the tone C—the generator tone in our case—at the top.The result will be the common diagram known as the Cycle/ Circle of the Fifths, as shown herein. From the note C (Do), we progress three times in each direction to reach the seven tones of the diatonic scale.

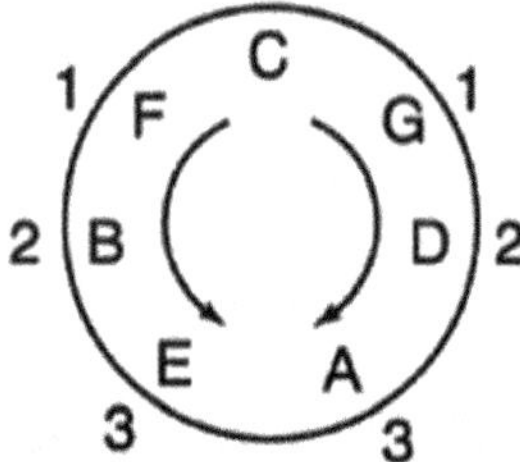

Harmonic progression along the cycle of Perfect Fifths is the most natural, and a succession of harmonies not in this relation has the character of a delay or suspension of this natural progression. From only one given Fifth flows the whole musical system, which naturally must be in the same proportion as the first. There was no tampering with this proportion and no substitution for another one.

The progression by the Fifths to reach the seven tones of the diatonic scale, as illustrated herein, shows us that the generated (self-producing) Fifths never coincide with the progressing octaves.

The keyboard, however, cannot give us the true representation of the relationship between the progression of fifths and octaves. We therefore must follow the example shown on the monochord, where it is shown that the Perfect Fifth is produced by 2/3 of the total length of the string and the octave at ½ of its length.

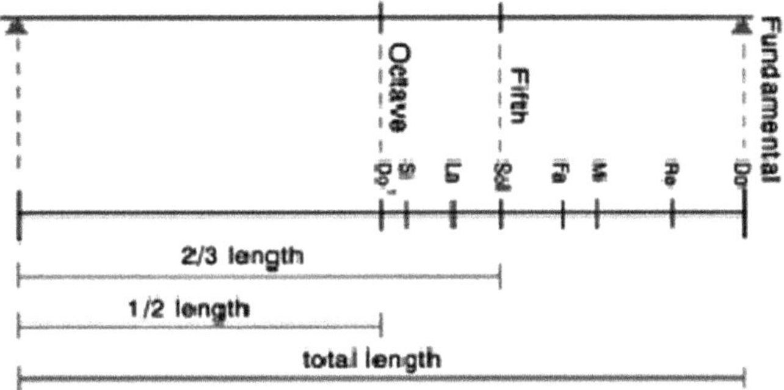

A progression by Perfect Fifths will mean finding the next Perfect Fifth at 2/3 of the original 2/3 of the length, etc. It is easy to see that any progress in fifths means multiplying the ratio 2:3 by itself, and no power of 3 can ever coincide with a power of 2, which the octave requires.

We continue expanding by the fifths in both directions (up and down the scale). The successive transpositions of the scale produce numerous sharps and flats, arranged by fifths. The cycle of the self-producing Perfect Fifths are plotted along its length/circumference—the string is imagined to be looped in the form of a circle.

It was found that after 53 natural Fifths, any new Fifth expediently coincides with a prior existing Fifth. The increment between the 53 natural Fifths was/is called a comma. Accordingly, the Egyptians defined the tone system, with reference to the Circle of Fifths, on the basis of the unit of measure known as the comma, by subdividing the octave into 53 equal steps. This comma has a value of 22.6415 cents. (A cent is a standard unit for measuring musical intervals. An octave is equal to 1,200 cents.)

It is interesting to note that the European treatises of the Middle Ages refer to this particular comma of 22.6415 cents as an "Arabian Comma", even though no Arabian written documentation in the Arabized world ever mentioned it or used it—except for the "Arabic speaking" people of Egypt. As such, it can only be and was/is an Egyptian comma.

Analysis of Ancient Egyptian instruments is consistent with multiples of the Egyptian comma.

Each Egyptian comma consists of three equal parts which the Egyptians called/call buk-nunu—meaning 'the mouth of the baby'. This was/is an Egyptian term and not Arabic one (a baby's mouth in Arabic is Fam El Radee-a). It should be noted that the division into thirds is consistent with the concept of the Fifth, since 2/3 of a comma is the Fifth within the comma.

The three buk-nunu in a comma are to be considered the Three-in-One—the Egyptian concept of trinity [read more about this subject in *Egyptian Cosmology: the Animated Universe,* by same author].

Analysis of the holes in found Ancient Egyptian wind instruments and frets on found string instruments, as well as the ratio of string lengths in the harps, proves with consistency the use of these "unique" discreet increments of the Egyptian comma and buk-nunu. An example is a common Ancient Egyptian interval of 11:12, which is equivalent to 151 cents (6 2/3 commas = 20 buknunus). [More examples are found in *The Enduring Ancient Egyptian Musical System* or its older edition *Egyptian Rhythm*, both by Moustafa Gadalla.]

7.2 AFFIRMATION OF SIGNIFICANCE OF COMMA FROM MUSICAL INSTRUMENTS

The Egyptian musical comma is an inevitable natural result of tuning and playing stringed musical instruments. Stringed instruments are basically tuned in two ways:

1. The cyclic (up and down) method, which applies to open (unstopped) strings of the instrument, yields Perfect Fourths and Perfect Fifths.

   Tuning is done by selecting a string (C) and tuning another string to its upper Perfect Fifth (G), then reverting to (D) a Fourth down, and going up to (A) by another Fifth, and so on. This difference between a Fifth and a Fourth is called a major whole tone, which is equal to 203.77 cents (i.e. nine Egyptian commas).

2. The divisive method is utilized to tune instruments with defined necks (like a guitar). Tuning is accomplished by stopping strings along the neck at proportioned distances (by use of frets), as follows:

   $^1/_2$ the length to get the Octave
   $^1/_3$ the length to get the Fifth
   $^1/_4$ the length to get the Fourth

When comparing the string vibrations of these two methods of tuning stringed instruments, we are faced with the following results:

	Cyclic	Divisive
C-D	203.77 cents (9 commas)	203.77 cents (9 commas)
D-E	203.77 cents (9 commas)	181.13 cents (8 commas)
E-F	90.56 cents (4 commas)	113.21 cents (5 commas)
Total:	498.11 cents	498.11 cents

The two tuning types show differences between D–E and E–F. The difference between the two methods yields two sizes of a whole tone (203.77 and 181.13 cents) and two sizes of semitone (90.56 and 113.21 cents). The difference between the two sizes is the Egyptian comma, for each of the intervals D–E and E–F.

The Egyptian orchestra tunes both types (cyclic and divisive) of string instruments by using the Egyptian qanoon (zither), which is the instrument that other instruments in the orchestra tune to, because it follows both principles at once: it has open strings that follow the cyclic system of tuning, while the melody string follows the divisive system. The melody string is fretted not by actual raised frets, but by marking the stopping places along the soundboard. [More about the qanoon in *The Enduring Ancient Egyptian Musical System* by Moustafa Gadalla.]

7.3 "WILLFUL ALTERNATION OF NATURE"!

We have shown above that the Egyptian comma explains both the Siamese twin nature of tones and the divergence in tuning results of musical stringed instruments.

Western musicologists considered the comma to be a mistake of creation that must be corrected. Curt Sachs, in his book *Our Musical Heritage* [pages 15-16], states:

> ***"The irreconcilable divergence between the two methods (cyclic and divisive) harassed the music of the West no less than that of the East, until the equal temperament, or division of the octave into twelve equal semitones, at last did away in the 18th century with the dubious so-called 'natural' intervals.***
>
> ***Temperament, or tuning compromise, in some form, however, is neither a western nor a modern achievement. It exists everywhere and in every time, now as a spontaneous, now as a willful alteration of nature."***

This "willful alteration of nature" resulted from the notion that simple arithmetic must overrule the beauty of natural sounds.

The "simplification" of numbers is reflected now in the so-called "tempered" scale, whereby, as per Alexander J. Ellis' [19th century] system, the whole octave of 1,200 cents is divided into 12 equal semitones, each equal to 100 cents. Thus:

A semitone has	100 cents
A wholetone	200 cents
A minor third	300 cents
A major third	400 cents
A fourth	500 cents
A tritone (Augmented fourth)	600 cents
A fifth	700 cents
A minor sixth	800 cents
A major sixth	900 cents
A minor seventh	1000 cents
A major seventh	1100 cents
An octave	1200 cents

The above statement by Curt Sachs is incorrect, since:

1. Only those Western musicologists since the 19th century were/are "harassed" by the musical unit of the comma.

2. The term 'tempering' should be replaced by 'tinkering' or 'fudging' numbers. This process did not change the fact that the Fifth (for example) is only perfect at 702 cents. Anything different than the natural sound value (say, 700 cents for the Fifth) is not balanced.

In order for Western musicologists to write about the true natural musical tones, they came up with numerous and cumbersome terms; all of which can be reduced to multiples of the (one and only) Egyptian comma, such as:

1. minor semitone or leimmas of 90.56 cents = 4 commas
2. major semitone or apotomes of 113.21 cents = 5 commas
3. minor whole tone of 181.13 cents = 8 commas
4. major whole tone of 203.77 cents = 9 commas
5. natural Fourth of 498.11 cents = 22 commas
6. natural Fifth of 701.89 cents = 31 commas

7.4 THE PHONEME PHENOMENA

The "unique" discreet increment of the Egyptian musical comma and its triple parts of buk-nunu have similar equivalence in the tonality of generative phonology.

Upon careful observation, we find that the sound of a particular letter will change, depending on the location of the letter in the word as well as its relationship to letters preceding and following it. An example in English is found in the articulations *tea, tie, toe,* and *two,* and yet is not identical with any of them.

These highly idealized, abstract patterns are called *phonemes*.

A phoneme may be defined operationally as representing the sound segment which, when changed by the substitution of another sound segment, changes the meaning and sound shape of a word.

The phoneme, as the smallest acoustic value, enables us to recognize and distinguish the sound shades of a letter/musical note.

There is generally a close correspondence between the letters and phonemes of a given language, but it is hardly exact in any language—except in the Egyptian system, where there are more phonemes than letters, which allows for the 4 sound variations of each letter by using more than one phoneme.

The various tonalities of each letter was/is reflected in the Egyptian writing system. Letters each can have up to four forms:

- Detached—the letter as it appears by itself, no letters joining to it either before or after.
- Initial—the letter as it appears when not preceded by a joining letter.
- Medial—the letter as it appears when there are joining letters both before and after the letter.
- Terminal—the letter as it appears when it is preceded, but not followed by joining letters.

Chapter 8 : The Musical Rhythmic Sound Segmentation—Syllabic

8.1 SEGMENTATION OF ORDERLY SOUND SEQUENCE [SYLLABLES]

Earlier we talked about individual sounds which are linguistically known as phonetics. Here we talk about the organization of sounds in a linguistic system—the way these sounds are distributed in utterance, which is known linguistically as phonology.

Phonology is based on phonetics and uses the same terminology and symbols.

The purpose of this chapter is to investigate the distribution of sounds in the Egyptian language and how such distribution system is intimately related to the same musical sound distribution system(s).

Each speech sound is characterized by its set of segmental features. When a group of sounds is articulated in continuous speech the continuous stream of speech reveals:

A. Individual sound segments—syllables
B. An organized Flow of Syllables Stream

It should be noted that the syllable, which combines important stress, rhythm, tempo, junctural, and phonotactic cues, is a key unit for the motor organization of speech.

In this subchapter, we will talk about point (A) and in the following subchapter we will deal with point (B).

We begin first with the syllables' significance, structure and forms.

After the letter phonemes in the speech sound or segment, the syllable is the next higher unit of the phonological and physiological integration of speech.

Most people have an intuitive "feel" for what a syllable is, but it is notoriously difficult to unambiguously define this unit.

Syllables also appear to be the smallest speech unit that can be stressed.

A syllable can be open (ended by a vowel) or closed (ended by a consonant).

- open: C[onsonant] V[owel];
- closed: CVC where the last (C) is marked with a vocalic sign called '*sukoon*' (meaning stoppage/ silence)—the lack of vowel after a consonant.

The simplest syllable structure is the "open" syllable shape, with a consonantal onset and a glottal stop or breathy offset. There are three basic types of open syllables:

1. Short syllables have the form consonant + short vowel and are followed by a short consonant in the next syllable.

2. Interrupted syllables are short vowels with the short vowel pronounced with great rapidity.

3. Long syllables have a consonant, plus either a long vowel or a short vowel, followed by one long consonant or by two short consonants.

The absolute duration of the sound of a syllable is called its quantity. In order to compare the quantity of any syllable with that of another, it is convenient to link both to some standard. This standard is called the short syllable, and is presumed to be the shortest sound which a man can utter distinctly. The unit of measurement used is the eighth note and was defined the "first time" as an ultimate atom which could not be divided by either a syllable or a note or a gesture.

The metric accents in both poetry and melody followed the quantitative principle—the length of a syllable/note.

This theory is so grounded in nature that the whole of Ancient Egyptian versification is founded upon it. They managed to keep up, in each word, the duration of each syllable distinct from its accent, which is like speaking in a regular musical singsong.

The long vowels are exactly like the short ones, but are held longer in pronunciation – some say "twice as much time". Actually, it can be held for as long is desired. The duration is measured (and marked) as multiple of the standard time for a short vowel.

In non-singing applications, long syllables take approximately twice as long to say as do short ones, and this gives Egyptian a characteristic "stacatto" rhythm. The same exact thing occurred in Ancient Egypt.

A system of marking vowels by the use of supralinear and sublinear marks were [and continue to be] utilized. Egyptian short vowels are generally not written, except sometimes in sacred texts and didactics, which are known as vocalized texts. Short vowels may be written with diacritics placed above or below the consonant that precedes them in the syllable. In verse text (and, very occasionally indeed, in prose) a scribe may mark the quantity of a long or short syllable with plural stroke(s).

It should be noted that the basic signs were derived from letters of the alphabet and were written in very small script above or below the consonant after which the vowel sound was to be pronounced. The three primary signs were/are associated with the three quantal vowels [see Chapter 4].

All true music proceeds from these three primary accents/tonal sounds.

The three accents—acute, grave and circumflex—were/are the symbols of tonal inflections which were/are essential qualities of the Egyptian language. They help the pitch level be high, medium, low, rising, or falling.

It should be recognized that accents are basically the same

as duration: i.e. they represent an increase in the length of the syllable.

It has been noted by all Egyptologists that not only is every Egyptian word stressed, but every syllable bears a relatively higher or lower stress, and they endeavor to express this stress by conventional accentual marks.

Accents are rarely written in prose literature, but they are likely to be used fairly frequently in texts of lyric verse. In such cases, their presence may help the reader to divide the words correctly.

Accentual marks indicate the tone syllable in each word and, besides, serve to indicate pauses and also the logical connections between words and clauses. Still another function of this comprehensive system of accents was to serve as a musical notation governing the modulations of liturgical chant in temple services.

8.2. ORGANIZED FLOW OF SYLLABLES STREAM

We have already dealt with both the syllables' significance and their structure and forms. Now we turn our attention to the syllables' streams, boundaries and tempo (rate).

It should be clear that the syllable which combines important stress, rhythm, tempo, junctural, and phonotactic cues is a key unit for the motor organization of speech.

As soon as we begin to connect two syllables together, we perceive that there is something which gives more prominence to one than to another. We do not pronounce each one of a collection of syllables (which collectively have one single meaning) with precisely the same force or intensity. We may observe a similar effect in music: certain notes in a musical passage will be distinguished from the rest by having a stress laid upon them, without any alteration in their pitch or time of duration. This stress is merely a greater degree of loudness.

A single syllable or a collection of syllables will constitute a word when they are spoken in invariable connection, and in such connection represent one or more ideas which are as invariably connected in the mind of the speaker; provided that, if the collection consists of more than one syllable, there be always some syllable which is distinguished from the rest by a stress laid upon it, or by the loudness with which it is spoken. That is, every word must have an accent upon one of its syllables.

Although the loudness with which one syllable is spoken must always predominate in a collection of syllables constituting a word, the remaining syllables may be pronounced with very different degrees of loudness. A certain degree is necessary in order that any sound should exist. If we call the loudest syllable the accented syllable, then the next in loudness is said to have a secondary accent, the next a tertiary, and so on; but that pronounced with the least degree of loudness in each word is generally said to be unaccented; a term which must be understood relatively and not absolutely.

Very few words, and only those very long ones, have more than two accents. In order to express the arrangement of accents in a word, the method employed consists of using the numbers 1, 2, and 3 for the primary, secondary, and tertiary accent, and 0 for the absence of accent, so that the numbers 1, 2, and 3 are nearly in the inverse proportion of the loudness with which a syllable is uttered.

Rhythm is the distribution of stress across the syllable train. This can be illustrated as follows: the numbers 1 to 6 represent syllables. If stressed, they are uppercase; if not, lowercase. Read the numbers, raising your voice to emphasize each uppercase example and lowering your voice for each lowercase (unstressed):

> 123456 Every other syllable is stressed
> 123456 Every third syllable is stressed
> 123456 Every syllable receives equal stress

The stream of syllables has both a rate and a rhythm. The tempo (rate) at which continuous speech is produced is commonly measured by measuring the number of syllables spoken per second. Thus, syllables appear to be a natural unit for the estimation of speech tempo.

Syllables are separated from each other by potential boundary signals called junctures. Juncturing is the process whereby a speaker inserts acoustic cues into the stream of speech, separating syllables, words, and phrases. Since every utterance can be broken into a stream of syllables, all higher-level juncture boundaries between words, phrases, clauses, and sentences occur at syllable junctures. These boundaries are often, but not always, marked by pauses, variations in vocal pitch and intensity, and other signals.

The rhythmical values in the transcriptions follow the metrical values of the syllables unless the rhythmical notation calls for something different. As a rule, the text accompanying the musical transcriptions has been divided into syllables without regard to the norm of syllabification in order to distinguish metrically open and closed syllables.

If juncture boundary signals are used, they may be one of several diverse cues. For example, boundaries may be marked with silent pauses, with a lowered vocal frequency or vocal fry (glottal pulsing), or by the use of different allophones for the sounds adjacent to the juncture. A variety of separation indicators were used for various musical purposes, the details of which are beyond the scope of this book.

Chapter 9 : The Triad Generative Nucleus of Music/Language

9.1 THE TRIAD GENERATIVE NUCLEUS OF MUSIC/LANGUAGE

All Egyptologists who studied the morphology of Ancient Egyptian words since their earliest history (such as Alan Gardiner, Kurt Sethe, etc.) testified that the archetypal building block in the Egyptian language is the stem verb that consists of 3 letters that contain the essence of the word's meaning.

Such a stem verb, consisting of 3 consonants, is the core of certain aspects/actions that germinate into various related grammatical meanings. The same exact rule applies to musical compositions.

It should be noted also that all Ancient Egyptian verb stems consist of only 3 radicals. The number 3 represents the building block in all aspects of the created universe, and the Ancient Egyptian language represents such a fundamental principle.

The root of each word establishes its character, for it is of the same nature, temper, constitution, or genius. The root is an independent entity. The character is a dependent entity; a manifestation of its root. It is of like nature or of peculiar constitution, attributable to its root. The properties of a character must agree with its word root as a property of that word root and as an offspring, expressing it by its noticeable likeness to it. The word speaks. The literate characters give the sound and substance.

In the Egyptian language, the three-letter root stem verb form the basis of morphology. Similarly, the musical triad is the root of any musical composition. Both the trilateral stem verbs and the musical triads follow the same exact composition, featuring grammatical rules of composition.

9.2 INVERSION/SHUFFLING OF TRIAD GENERATIVE NUCLEUS

Each letter/musical note has its own specific vibrational pattern. The meaning of a trilateral stem verb emerges from the arrangements of its three letters, as the meaning of a chord results from the arrangements of its musical notes.

When reshuffling the order of the musical triad, we sometimes end up with another triad—but some of the reordered arrangements do not sound right; i.e. they are meaningless. The same exact thing is found in the Egyptian language. Take, for example, the word H.SB (meaning 'to reckon') and reshuffle it to:

- H.BS means to apprehend
- SBH.—to swim
- SH.B—to draw

– BSH.—has no meaning—unworkable musical triad
– BH.S—has no meaning—unworkable musical triad

9.3 GERMINATION OF THE GENERATIVE NUCLEUS

The British Egyptologist Alan Gardiner, in his book *Egyptian Grammar,* on page 208, states unequivocally:

> ***"The existence of germinating verbs in Egyptian is established beyond a doubt"***

Words in the Egyptian language are formed from roots by the addition of (unwritten) vowels, prefixes, infixes, or suffixes according to certain fixed patterns. For example, using the radicals h. -s-b (both an Ancient Egyptian and an Arabic word), it is theoretically possible to derive as many as 14 new verbs and scores of nouns.

Both the tri-consonantal root verb (and its rich derivatives) and the varied sounds of vowels that change the grammatical character of the word make this language very poetic, powerful, expressive, energetic, and easy for everyone to use to compose poetry, puns, word plays, etc.

Conjugation is effected by means of prefixes, infixes, and suffixes, all added to the stem.

– The prefixes consist of the augment and reduplication,
– the infixes in the tense character and mood vowel; and
– the suffixes in the person endings.

Everything stated above about verb germination applies to musical compositions by working around musical triads.

Chapter 10 : Composition Affinities of Music and Language

10.1 COMPOSITION—FUNCTIONS AND FORMS

The composition of a melody/mode must follow certain design criteria in order to meet the desired objective. This fact was first known and implemented in Ancient Egypt.

In the 4th century BCE, Plato recommended that the Ideal State be erected upon the foundation of music, a well-established system based on a theory of the ethos of music as a theory of the psycho-physiological effects of music on the State and on man. Plato's recommendation was the adoption of Ancient Egypt's system and practices, as stated in Plato's *Collected Dialogues*, in *Laws II* [656c–657c]:

> ***"ATHENIAN: Then is it conceivable that anywhere where there are, or may hereafter be, sound laws in force touching this educative-playful function of the Muses, men of poetic gifts should be free to take whatever in the way of rhythm, melody, or diction tickles the composer's fancy in the act of composition and teach it through the choirs to the boys and lads of a***

law-respecting society, leaving it to chance whether the result prove virtue or vice?

CLINIAS: To be sure, that does not sound rational decidedly not.

ATHENIAN: And yet this is precisely what they are actually left free to do, I may say, in every community with the exception of Egypt.

CLINIAS: And in Egypt itself, now—pray how has the law regulated the matter there?

ATHENIAN: The mere report will surprise you. That nation (Egypt), it would seem, long enough ago recognized the truth we are now affirming, that poses and melodies must be good, if they are to be habitually practiced by the youthful generation of citizens. So they (Egyptians) drew up the inventory of all the standard types, and consecrated specimens of them in their temples....

ATHENIAN: . . .in this matter of music in Egypt, it is a fact, and a thought-provoking fact, that it has actually proved possible, in such a sphere, to canonize melodies which exhibit an intrinsic rightness permanently by law. . . .

So, as I was saying before, if we can but detect the intrinsically right in such matters, in whatever degree, we should reduce them to law and system without misgiving, since the appeal to feeling which shows itself in the perpetual craving for novel musical sensation can, after all, do comparatively little to corrupt choric art,

once it has been consecrated, by deriding it as out of fashion. In Egypt, at any rate, its corrupting influence appears to have been no-wise potent, but very much the reverse.

CLINIAS: That seems to be the state of the case from your present account.

ATHENIAN: Then may we say boldly that the right way to employ music and the recreations of the choric art is on some such lines as these? When we believe things are going well with us, we feel delight, and, conversely, when we feel delight we believe things are well with us".

The above scripts from Plato's *Collected Dialogues* show how the Greeks considered Ancient Egypt to be the sole source of their Ideal Laws, as related to music (among other things). The Greek text above admits the following:

1. Only Egypt had sound laws that govern melodies and poses.

2. Only Egypt had an inventory of well-designed standard type modes/melodies and the regulations by which they are performed—time, place, and occasion.

3. Only Egypt had practiced their prescribed Ideal Laws for music, dance, poetry, etc.

The very same functions and forms apply to written and vocalic language. Sentences/verses are classified in accordance with the different kinds of intention which they embody; for every sentence must embody some intention on the part of the speaker/writer/singer.

The Egyptian language had/has a set grammatical rules and corresponding words orders. However, variations from these set rules were obligatory when it came to word order, in order to provide the intended intent, as noted by Alan Gardiner in his book *Egyptian Grammar*, on page 413:

> ***"Syntactical position of words is not tied down to fixed and definite rules, as is the case with English and other modern languages. Therefore a sentence like the father loves his son may be expressed according as the stress lies on this or that word."***

The very same rules of word orders apply in musical arrangements/compositions.

The natural flow of musical composition follows the same patterns of sentences. Having combined our elementary sounds into syllables, and by combining syllables into words by the addition of other syllables when necessary, we may proceed to join words into sentences.

As a primarily accented syllable predominates over all the others in the same word, so an emphatic word predominates over all the others in the same clause; and as there may be words with a primary, secondary, tertiary, etc. accent, so there may be clauses with a primary, secondary, tertiary, etc. emphasis. Each collection of words terminated by a slight pause has, however, one word which is more emphatic than all the rest. If every virtual word in the language—substantive, adjective, verb, etc.—had only one strongly accented vowel, then every Egyptian line of verse would have had two to four accentuations, with optional depressions between.

This alternating nature between long/strong and short/weak syllables has its counterpart (or, more accurately, roots) in music; for each musical scale-octave has two centers—one weak and the other strong.

And just like musical compositions, Egyptian sentences may be simple or multiple. Multiple sentences are joined in various ways such as simple connectivity, overlapping, or concord by the assimilation of one element of a sentence or clause to another in some important particular of form.

The normal musical sentence is that of eight measures, frequently (but not necessarily) divided into two half-sentences of four measures each. There are other sentences or phrases that are shorter and longer. These are brought about by omissions or overlappings or by extensions, repetitions, or expansions. Eight measures is the norm. Likewise, the octave-scale, whether diatonic, chromatic, or enharmonic, always consisted of eight notes and no more—either as two disjoined tetrachords, or joined + 1 note, or overlapping tetrachords + additional notes—but always eight notes to the octave. With these variations, some scales were tense and others relaxed, some disjunct and others conjunct, some pure and others mixed, some "plagal" and others "authentic", and some denoted structures and others keys—just to mention a few of the endless possibilities.

There are numerous aspects to be considered in musical composition. This book will not get into all their details.

10.2 MUSICAL FORMS/THEMES OF POETRY

The Egyptians perceived language and music as two sides of the same coin. Both poetry and singing followed similar rules for musical composition. Poetry is written not only with a rhyme scheme, but also with a recurring pattern of accented and unaccented syllables. Each syllable alternates between accented and unaccented, making a double/quadruple meter and several other varieties. Patterns of set rhythms or lengths of phrases of Ancient Egyptian poems, praises, hymns, and songs of all kinds, which are known to have been chanted or performed with some musical accompaniment, were rhythmic, with uniform meters and a structured rhyme.

The themes and metrics of lyrical poetry are the same in both Ancient and present-day Egypt. The most common copla is an octosyllabic quartet with loose, alternate rhyme. Many are composed of three, five, and six lines of varying syllabic lengths. The singer often repeats and lengthens lines, depending on the traditional vocal ornaments of a given style. Likewise, the Ancient (and present-day Baladi) Egyptian poetry has had the same exact structural forms and artistic features.

Everything that the Egyptian writes (whatever the subject is) falls into short lines of approximately equal length. These lines have a verse; i.e. some sort of metrical structure. This is, in many cases, a fixed number of lines—generally there are three or four—that belong together. Four or double-fours are most common. There was/is also the stanza of a freer structure, the sections in which are of varying length, and display no regularity with regard to the number of lines.

Artistic rhythms, naturalness, brilliancy, and the charm of Egyptian poetry strives on wordplay, alliterations, tropes, and puns.

The following is a summary of the various forms/styles of poetry that are found in both Ancient and present-day Baladi Egypt:

1. The parallelism of the phrases, where two short sentences follow each other and correspond in arrangement and also as a rule in purport.

2. The parallel phrases may group themselves in strophes, as is shown in numerous poems. These parallel phrases are, moreover, frequently arranged in different order.

3. The antithetical style of poetry.

4. Alliterative style was used as a definite poetic form.

5. Poetry of a metrical nature—poetry divided into short lines, which were distinguished in the manuscripts by red dots. These little verses are punctuated not merely so as to denote their sense, but also for the divisions that are to be observed in recitation. Each verse contains a certain number of primary accents—usually two. The peculiar law of accentuation in the Egyptian language—that several words closely allied in syntax should be invested

with one primary accent—lies at the root of this verse construction.

Strophic poetry were accentual and divided into stanzas, such as:

- The muwashshah is a group of rhyming phrases molded into a pattern that consists of strophes. The outstanding feature of the genre (the one to which it owes its name of muwashshah) is the regular alternation between two elements: lines with separate rhymes and others with common rhymes. Meter is not an essential feature.

  The antecedents of the muwashshah were to be sought in the same strophic poetry known in Ancient Egypt as musammat, which is a poem of very simple metrical structure. It consisted of several lines—usually three or four—with a common rhyme followed by one with a separate rhyme. The scheme of a poem having strophes of four verses (murabba') will thus be: aaaB cccB, and that of one with strophes of five verses (mukhammas): aaaaB ccccB.

  The Ancient Egyptian texts provide an extensive number and variety of musammat/muwashshahat in the forms of litanies, rosaries, eulogies, psalms, hymns, etc. Likewise, present-day Egyptian mystics (Sufis) utilize the same ancient poetic and recitative compositions. Egyptian mystics have a countless number of these poetic and musical compositions that they know by heart. The mystical rosaries (awrad) are usually a long, well-composed series in the form of poetic stanzas of recitations. Each rosary consists of well-designed components/sections, each with their own particular climaxes. These rosaries are replete with wise proverbial sayings, pious reflections, and moral precepts. These hundreds of Egyptian compositions are too old to be accredited to specific authors.

1

GLOSSARY

Animism – The concept that all things in the universe are animated (energized) by life forces. This concurs, scientifically, with kinetic theory, where each minute particle of any matter is in constant motion, energized with life forces.

aspirated – Marked by release of a puff of air. Example: English p is aspirated in pie, unaspirated in spy.

attributes – the Divine qualities and meanings that are the real causative factors of the manifested creations.

Baladi – local, a term used to describe the present native silent majority in Egypt, which adheres to the Ancient Egyptian traditions, under a thin layer of Islam.

BCE – Before Common Era. Also noted in other references as BC.

beat – a constant pulsation. It acts as a ruler by which we can measure time.

Book of Coming Forth By Light (Per-em-hru) – consists of over 100 chapters of varying lengths, which are closely related to the Unas Transformational/Funerary (so-called Pyramid) Texts at Saqqara. This book is only found, in its complete form, on papyrus scrolls that were wrapped in the mummy swathing of the deceased and buried with him.

buk-nunu – an Ancient Egyptian musical unit, equal to 7.55 cents.

CE – Common Era. Also noted in other references as AD.

cent – a standard unit for measuring musical intervals. An octave is equal to 1,200 cents.

chironomid – one who gestures with his/her hands—a maestro/conductor.

chironomy – the art of conducting or representing music by gestures of the fingers, hand(s), and/or arm(s).

chord – a combination of three or more tones sounded together in harmony.

comma – an Ancient Egyptian musical unit, equal to 22.64 cents. See comma in Index for more information and details.

cosmology – The study of the origin, creation, structure, and orderly operation of the universe as a whole, and of its related parts.

diatonic – A scale consisting of 5 whole tones and 2 semitones (from the 3rd to the 4th, and from the 7th to the octave).

Duat/Tuat — (Ancient Egypt) The Underworld, where the soul goes through transformation, leading to resurrection.

enharmonic – designating a ¼ step/note or less.

ethos – the expression of a mode that is connected to its structure. Describes the ethical power or moral force of a mode and its ability to influence the development of character and attitudes in the listener.

Fifth, Perfect – can mean either: 1) the natural sound of the fifth tone of an ascending diatonic scale, or a natural tone four degrees above or below any given natural-sounding tone in such a scale—dominant. 2) the interval between two such natural-sounding tones, or a combination of them.

Fourth – can mean either: 1) the fourth tone of an ascending diatonic scale, or a tone three degrees above or below any given tone in such a scale—subdominant. 2) the interval between two such tones, or a combination of them.

halftone – see **semitone**.

heptatonic – consists of seven (hepta) tones.

interval – can mean either: 1) the ratio of the number of vibrations between two different tones. 2) The distance separating two consecutive musical notes. [Also see **tone** and **semitone**.]

mysticism – consists of ideas and practices that lead to union with the Divine. Union is described more accurately as togetherness, joining, arriving, conjunction, and the realization of God's uniqueness.

meter – succession of equal beats, characterized by the periodic return of a strong beat.

mode – a rhythmical system consisting of its own unique combination of tones and rhythms, in order to specifically influence the listener. [Also see **ethos**.]

monophonemic – refers to systems in which there are separate symbols for individual phonemes.

neter/netert – a divine principle/function/attribute of the One Great God. (Incorrectly translated as god/goddess).

notes – in Western musical terms, the letters A (La) to G (Sol) are used to designate notes.

onomatopoeic – the naming of a thing or action by a vocal imitation of sound associated with it (example: hiss).

papyrus – could mean either: 1) A plant that is used to make a writing surface. 2) Paper, as a writing medium. 3) The text written on it, such as "Leiden Papyrus".

pentatonic – a scale consisting of five tones—three of which are whole tones, and two semitones—like that of the black keys on a keyboard.

perfect – the name given to certain intervals—the Fourth,

Fifth, and Octave. The term is applied to these intervals in their natural sounds (not "tempered").

Phonetic Complement/Indicator – A sign expressing a phonetic but non-semantic element above/below/attached to the basic letter.

Phonography – A full writing – that is: a system of signs expressing linguistic elements by means of visible marks.

pitch – the position of a tone in a musical scale, determined by the frequency of vibration and measured by cycles per second.

polyphony – the simultaneous sounding of different notes; the sounding of two or more different melodies simultaneously.

polymorphemic – refers to single symbols which stand for all the phonemes in a syllable.

"Pyramid" Texts – a collection of transformational (funerary) literature that was found in the tombs of the 5th and 6th Dynasties (2465-2150 BCE).

scales – any series of eight tones to the octave, arranged in a step-by-step rising or falling of pitch, which consists of a given pattern of intervals (the differences of pitch between notes). Conventional music relies on the use of scales, which consist of a given pattern of intervals (the differences of pitch between notes). These intervals are described in terms of tones, semitones, and smaller measurements. The most common scales are: diatonic, chromatic, and enharmonic.

semitone – the intervals between B (Si) and C (Do), and between E (Mi) and F (Fa). [Also see **tone.**]

Sign, Phonetic – Any sign of a full writing which expresses linguistic elements by means of visible marks, such as an Alphabetic, Syllabic and Word Sign, and, in some systems, a Prosodic and Phrase Sign. Phonetic Signs may be subdivided into two classes: (1) Phonetic semantic signs, such as word and phrase signs, (2) phonetic non-semantic signs, such as alphabetic, syllabic, and prosodic signs.

Sign, Prosodic – A sign or mark to denote a prosodic feature, such as quantity, accent, tone, and pause.

stanza – a group of lines of verse forming one of the divisions of a poem or song. It typically has a regular pattern in the number of lines and the arrangement of meter and rhyme.

stele (plural: stelae) – a stone or wooden slab or column inscribed with commemorative texts.

step – interval of sound.

temperament – the rounding off of the values of musical intervals away from those of their natural values, to the nearest 100 cent number. Keyboard instruments are tuned to a scale of equal "temperament".

tetrachord – a series of four tones comprising the total interval of a Perfect Fourth; half an octave.

Thoth – represents the Divine aspects of wisdom and intellect. It was Thoth who uttered the words that created the world, as commanded by Re. He is represented as the messenger of the neteru (gods/goddesses) of writing, language, and knowledge.

timbre – the quality or color of the sound invoked. It distinguishes one voice or instrument from another.

tone – the combination of pitch, intensity (loudness) and quality (timbre). The interval between each of the notes is a tone, except between B (Si) and C (Do) and between E (Mi) and F (Fa), where the interval is a semitone, in each case.

tonality – the relationship between musical sounds or tones, taking into account their vibratory relationships and their appreciation by the ear. A systematic musical structure.

unison – the same sound, produced by two or more instruments or voices.

Writing – A system of communication by means of conventional visible marks.

2

SELECTED BIBLIOGRAPHY

Assmann, J. *Agyptische Hymnen Und Gebete* (*Leiden Papyrus* p. 312-321). Zürich/Münich, 1975.

Baines, John and Jaromir Málek. *Atlas of Ancient Egypt.* New York, 1994.

Breasted, James Henry. *Ancient Records of Egypt*, 3 Vols. Chicago, USA, 1927.

Budge, Sir E. A. Wallis. *Egyptian Language: Easy Lessons in Egyptian Hieroglyphics*. New York, 1983.

Budge, E.A. Wallis. *Egyptian Religion: Egyptian Ideas of the Future Life*. London, 1975.

Burney, Charles. *A General History of Music*, 2 volumes. New York, 1935.

Chejne, Anwar G. *The Arabic Language: Its Role in History*. Minneapolis, Minnesota, USA, 1969.

Daniels, Peter T & Bright, William. *The World's Writing Systems.* Oxford, 1996.

Daniloff, Raymond; Schuckers, Gordon; and Feth, Lawrence. *The Physiology of Speech and Hearing*. Englewood Cliffs, NJ, USA, 1980.

Dio Cassius. *Roman History, Vol 3.* Tr. By E. Gary. London, 1914.

Diodorus of Sicily. *Books I, II, & IV*, tr. By C.H. Oldfather. London, 1964.

Driver, G.R. *Semitic Writing: from Pictograph to Alphabet*. London, 1954.

Drucker, Johanna. *The Alphabetic Labyrinth*. New York, 1995.

Egyptian Book of the Dead (The Book of Going Forth by Day), The Papyrus of Ani. USA, 1991.

Ellis, Alexander John. *The Alphabet of Nature*. 1845.

Engel, Carl. *The Music of The Most Ancient Nations*. London, 1929.

Erman, Adolf. *Life in Ancient Egypt*. New York, 1971.

Erman, Adolph. *The Literature of the Ancient Egyptians*, tr. by Aylward M. Blackman. London, 1927.

Fétis, François Joseph. *Biographie Universelle des Musiciens et Bibliographie Générale de la Musique. (Universal biography of Musicians)*. Bruxelles, 1837.

Findlen, Paula, Ed. *Athanasius Kircher: The Last Man Who Knew Everything*. New York, 2004.

Firmage, Richard A. *The Alphabet ABECEDARIUM: Some Notes on Letters*. Boston, 1993.

Gadalla, Moustafa:

- *Ancient Egyptian Culture Revealed*. USA, 2007.
- *Egyptian Cosmology: The Animated Universe—2nd edition*. USA, 2001.
- *Egyptian Divinities: The All Who Are THE ONE*. USA, 2001.
- *Egyptian Mystics: Seekers of the Way*. USA, 2003.
- *Egyptian Rhythm: The Heavenly Melodies*. USA, 2002.
- *Egyptian Romany: The Essence of Hispania*. USA, 2004.

Gardiner, Sir Alan. *Egyptian Grammar: Being an Introduction to the Study of Hieroglyphs*, 3rd ed. Oxford, 1994.

Gefin, Laszlo. *Ideogram: History of Poetic Method*. Austin, TX, USA, 1982.

Gelb, I.J. *A Study of Writing: The Foundation of Grammatology*. Chicago, IL, USA, 1952.

Gilsenan, Michael. *Saint and Sufi in Modern Egypt*. Oxford, 1973.

Godwin, Joscelyn. *Robert Fludd: Hermatic Philosopher and Surveyor of Two Worlds*. London, 1990.

Godwin, Joscelyn. *Athanasius Kircher: A Renaissance Man and the Quest for Lost Knowledge*. London, 1979.

Gretz, Ronald J. *Music Language and Fundamentals*. USA, 1994.

Healey, John F. *The Early Alphabet*. London, 1990.

Herodotus. *The Histories*. Tr. By Aubrey DeSelincourt. London, 1996.

Hickmann, Hans. *Musikgeschichte in Bildern: Ägypten*. Leipzig, Germany, 1961.

Hickmann, Hans. *Orientalische Musik*. Leiden, 1970.

Jensen, Hans. *Sign, Symbol and Script*. London, 1970.

Jensen, John T. *Principles of Generative Phonology*. Philadelphia, PA, USA, 2004.

Khaldûn, Ibn. *The Muqaddimah: An Introduction to History*, tr. From the Arabic by Franz Rosenthal, abridged and edited by N.J. Dawood. Princeton, 1969.

Lane, E.W. *The Manners and Customs of the Modern Egyptians*. London, 1836.

Levy, Ernst and Siegmund LeVarie. *Music Morphology – A discourse and dictionary*. Kent, Ohio, USA, 1983.

Levy, Ernst. *A Theory of Harmony. Albany*, New York, USA, 1985.

Petrie, W.M. Flinders. *The Formation of the Alphabet*. London, 1912.

Piankoff, Alexandre. *The Litany of Re*. New York, 1964.

Piankoff, Alexandre. *The Shrines of Tut-Ankh-Amon Texts*. New York, 1955.

Plato. *The Collected Dialogues of Plato including the Letters*. Edited by E. Hamilton & H. Cairns. New York, 1961.

Plutarch, *De Iside Et Osiride*. Tr. By J. Gwyn Griffiths. Wales, U.K., 1970.

Plutarch. *Plutarch's Moralia, Volume V.* Tr. by Frank Cole Babbitt. London, 1927.

Polin, Claire C. J. *Music of the Ancient Near East*. New York, 1954.

Roussier, Pierre Joseph. *Mémoire Sur La Musique Des Anciens.* Paris, 1770.

Sachs, Curt. *The History of Musical Instruments*. New York, 1940.

Sachs, Curt. *Our Musical Heritage.* Englwood Cliffs, NJ, USA, 1955.

Sachs, Curt. *Rhythm and Tempo: A Study in Music History*. New York, 1953.

Sachs, Curt. *The Rise of Music in the Ancient World.* New York,1943.

Sachs, Curt. *The Wellsprings of Music*. The Hague, Holland, 1962.

Shah, Idries. *The Sufis*. New York, 1964.

Sicilus, *Diodorus*. Vol 1. Tr. by C.H. Oldfather. London.

Subhan, John A. *Sufism: Its Saints and Shrines*. Lucknow [pref. 1938].

Taylor, Isaac. *The History of the Alphabet*, 2 vols. New York, 1899.

Touma, H.H. *The Music of the Arabs*. Portland, Oregon, USA, 1996.

Wilkinson, J. Gardner. *The Ancient Egyptians: Their Life and Customs*. London, 1988.

Several Internet sources.

Numerous references in Arabic language.

3

SOURCES & NOTES

References to sources in the previous section, Selected Bibliography, are only referred to for the facts, events, and dates—not for their interpretations of such information.

It should be noted that if a reference is made to one of the author Moustafa Gadalla's books, that each of his book contains appendices for its own extensive bibliography as well as detailed Sources and Notes.

Chapter 1: Historical Deception of the (Ancient) Egyptian Linguistics

1.1 Smoke Screening Thousands of Egyptian Alphabetical Writings: Gardiner

1.2 The (Ancient) Egyptian Alphabetical Form of Writing: Gadalla [Culture Revealed], Taylor, Vol. I, Plato, Erman [Literature], Petrie [Formation], Gardiner, Baines, Numerous references in Arabic language, Gadalla being an Egyptian native.

1.3 Egyptian is Dead—Long Live "Arabic": Gardiner, Numerous references in Arabic language, Gadalla being an Egyptian native.

Chapter 2: The Seamless Language and/of Music

2.1 Language and/of Music

– **Letters/Musical Notes:** Plato, Peacey, Sacks [Rise of Music], Stanford, Pohlmann, Drucker

– **Linguistic Uniformity—Speech/music:** Daniloff, Gadalla [Egyptian Romany]

– **The Orderly Flow of Sound Communications—Language:** Practically all references on the subject matter.

2.2 The Egyptian Tonal Writing System

– **Writing Components of The Egyptian Tonal Language:** Jensen, Daniels, Pohlmann, Gardiner, Assmann, Erman, Poli

– **Necessities of Phonetic Notations:** Gardiner, Drucker, Polin

– **Tonal Conformity Writing of Egyptian texts:** Burney, Vol. I, Turner, Stanford, Pohlmann, Gadalla [Culture Revealed], Gardiner, Drucker, Polin, Assmann, Erman

– **The Preeminence of Ancient Egyptian Tonal**

Writings: Plato, Fétis, Engel, Assmann, Gadalla [Egyptian Rhythm]

2.3 Significance of Musicality in Ancient Egypt: Sachs [Wellsprings], Gadalla [Egyptian Romany, Egyptian Mystics, Egyptian Rhythm]

Chapter 3: Human Vocal Instrument

3.1 Vocal Music Themes: Sachs [Wellsprings], Gadalla [Egyptian Rhythm]

3.2 Generating Vocal Sounds: Jensen, Burchett, Peacey, Plato, Levine, Gadalla [Egyptian Rhythm]

3.3 Human-Like Musical Instruments: Ellis, Daniloff, Gadalla [Egyptian Rhythm]

Chapter 4: The Three Primary Tonal Sounds

4.1 The Three Primary Rhythmic Tones: Diodorus, Gadalla [Egyptian Rhythm]

4.2 The Three Quantal Vowels/Sounds: Ellis, Jensen, Daniloff, Gadalla being an Egyptian native.

Chapter 5: The Musical/Tonal/Tonic Alphabets

5.1 Letters—Derivatives of the 3 Quantal Vowels: Ellis, Daniloff

5.2 The 25 Articulated Alphabetical/Musical Letters: Ellis, Plato, Firmage, Diodorus, Plutarch, Gadalla [Egyptian Rhythm]

5.3 Alphabetical Letters as Written Musical Notes:

Burney, Vol. I, Sacks [Rise of Music], Petrie [Formation], Pohlmann, Stanford, Fetis, Gadalla [Egyptian Rhythm]

Chapter 6: Duality of Letters/Musical Tones

6.1 Duality of Letters—Voiced and Unvoiced: Jensen, Burchett, Daniloff, Taylor, Vol. I, several Arabic references

6.2 Duality of Musical Tones—Authentic & Plagal: Sachs [Rise of Music], Gadalla [Egyptian Rhythm]

Chapter 7: The "Atom" of Musical/Vocal Sounds

7.1 The Musical Measuring Unit—Natural Progression: Sachs [Rise of Music], Gadalla [Egyptian Rhythm, Egyptian Cosmology]

7.2 Affirmation of Significance of Comma from Musical Instruments: Sachs [Rise of Music], Gadalla [Egyptian Rhythm]

7.3 "Willful Alternation of Nature"!: Sachs [Musical Heritage], Gadalla [Egyptian Rhythm]

7.4 The Phoneme Phenomena: Daniloff, Firmage, Taylor, Vol. I, Gadalla being an Egyptian native.

Chapter 8: The Musical Rhythmic Sound Segmentation—Syllabic

8.1 Segmentations of Orderly Sound Sequence [Syllables]: Jensen, Gardiner, Daniloff, Daniels, Ellis, Jannaris, Sacks [Rise of Music], Healey, Taylor, Vol.

I, Pohlman, Polin, Turner, Chejne, Gadalla being a native Egyptian.

8.2 Organized Flow of Syllables Stream: Daniloff, Erman [Literature], Gussenhoven, Pohlmann, Turner, Daniels, Gadalla [Egyptian Romany, Egyptian Rhythm]

Chapter 9: The Triad Generative Nucleus of Music/ Language

9.1 The Triad Generative Nucleus of Music/Language: Gardiner, Rasula, Gadalla [Egyptian Rhythm, Egyptian Romany], Gadalla being a native Egyptian.

9.2 Inversion/Shuffling of Triad Generative Nucleus: Gretz, Gadalla [Egyptian Rhythm], Gadalla being a native Egyptian.

9.3 Germination of The Generative Nucleus: Sacks [Rise of Music], Gardiner, Jannaris, Gadalla [Egyptian Romany]

Chapter 10: Composition Affinities of Music and Language

10.1 Composition—Functions and Forms

- **Moods and Modes:** Plato, Gardiner, Gadalla [Egyptian Rhythm]

- **Sentence Structures:** Jannaris, Gardiner, Ellis, Erman [Literature], Gadalla [Egyptian Rhythm]

- **Multiple Sentences:** Gardiner, Gadalla [Egyptian Rhythm]

- **Modes and Musical Structural Forms:** Gadalla [Egyptian Rhythm], Polin, Sacks [Rise of Music]

10.2 Musical Forms/Themes of Poetry: Gussenhoven, Gadalla [Egyptian Rhythm, Egyptian Romany]

www.ingramcontent.com/pod-product-compliance
Lightning Source LLC
LaVergne TN
LVHW010106110826
845155LV00028B/505